The First Noel

A DK PUBLISHING BOOK

Conceived by Miriam Farbey

Editors Nicholas Turpin and Marie Greenwood
Designer Ian Campbell
Picture research Andy Samson
Production Steve Lang
DTP Designer Kim Browne
Managing Art Editor Jacquie Gulliver
US Editor Constance M. Robinson

Music arranged by Lesley Applebee and Nigel Thomas

First American Edition, 1998
2 4 6 8 10 9 7 5 3

Published in the United States by DK Publishing, Inc., 95 Madison Avenue, New York, New York 10016
Visit us on the World Wide Web at http://www.dk.com

Published in Great Britain by Dorling Kindersley Limited.

Library of Congress Cataloging-in-Publication Data

The First Noel: A Child's book of Christmas carols to play and sing. — 1st American ed.
p.   cm.
Without the music.
Contents: O come, all ye faithful — We three kings of Orient are — Hark! the herald angels sing — Good King Wenceslas — Away in a
manger — The holly and the ivy — O little town of Bethlehem — The first Noel — Song of the crib — Silent Night — It came upon a
midnight clear — I saw three ships — We wish you a merry Christmas.
ISBN 0-7894-3483-0

1. Carols, English—Texts. 2. Christmas music—Texts. 3. Christmas in art.
M1999.F57 1998
782.28'1723'0268—dc21   98-23310
                                                          CIP
                                                          MN

Color reproduction by GRB Editrice, Italy
Printed and bound by Tien Wah Press in Singapore

The First Noel

A Child's Book of
 Christmas Carols
To Play and Sing

DK PUBLISHING, INC

INTRODUCTION

Christmas is a joyous time of year – a time for celebration, music, and good cheer. During the 19th century, when many carols were first composed, people often used to gather around the piano and sing. Today, people still love to sing Christmas carols, whether at church, in a concert hall, in the open air, or in the comfort of their own homes.

This collection combines thirteen favorite carols with richly evocative paintings of Christmases past and present to create a unique expression of the magic and mystery of Christmas.

CONTENTS

O Come all ye Faithful

Christmas Eve
 published by J. LATHAM, 1878

1. O come, all ye faithful,
   Joyful and triumphant,
   O come ye, O come ye to Bethlehem!
   Come and behold him,
   Born the King of angels!
   O come, let us adore him,
   O come, let us adore him,
   O come, let us adore him,
   Christ the Lord.

2. God of God,
   Light of Light,
   Lo! he abhors not the Virgin's womb;
   Very God,
   Begotten, not created. *Chorus*

3. Child, for us sinners,
   Poor and in the manger,
   Fain we embrace thee
       with love and awe;
   Who would not love thee,
   Loving us so dearly? *Chorus*

4. Sing, choirs of angels!
   Sing in exultation!
   Sing, all ye citizens of heaven above:
   Glory to God
   In the highest. *Chorus*

We Three Kings of Orient are

1. We three kings of Orient are;
   Bearing gifts, we traverse afar;
   Field and fountain, moor and mountain,
   Following yonder star.

   O star of wonder, star of night,
   Star with royal beauty bright,
   Westward leading, still proceeding,
   Guide us to thy perfect light.

2. Born a king on Bethlehem plain,
   Gold I bring to crown Him again –
   King forever, ceasing never
   Over us all to reign. *Chorus*

3. Frankincense to offer have I;
   Incense owns a Deity nigh;
   Prayer and praising all men raising,
   Worship him, God on high. *Chorus*

Three Kings
 by LINDA BENTON (Living artist)

4. Myrrh is mine; its bitter perfume
   Breathes a life of gathering gloom;
   Sorrowing, sighing, bleeding, dying,
   Sealed in the stone-cold tomb. *Chorus*

5. Glorious now, behold him arise,
   King, and God, and sacrifice.
   Heaven sings alleluia,
   Alleluia the earth replies. *Chorus*

Hark the Herald Angels Sing

The Angel of the Trumpet
 by Sir Edward Burne-Jones (1833–98)

1. Hark! the herald angels sing:
   Glory to the newborn King!
   Peace on earth, and mercy mild,
   God and sinners reconciled.
   Joyful, all ye nations rise,
   Join the triumph of the skies,
   With th'angelic host proclaim,
   "Christ is born in Bethlehem."
   Hark! the herald angels sing:
   Glory to the newborn King!

2. Christ, by highest heaven adored,
   Christ, the everlasting Lord,
   Late in time behold him come,
   Offspring of a Virgin's womb.
   Veiled in flesh the Godhead see,
   Hail, the incarnate Deity!
   Pleased as man with man to dwell,
   Jesus, our Emmanuel. *Chorus*

3. Mild he lays his glory by,
   Born that man no more may die,
   Born to raise the sons of earth,
   Born to give them second birth.
   Hail, the heaven-born Prince of Peace!
   Hail, the Sun of Righteousness!
   Light and life to all he brings,
   Risen with healing in his wings. *Chorus*

Good King Wenceslas

1. Good King Wenceslas looked out
   On the Feast of Stephen,
   When the snow lay round about,
   Deep and crisp and even.
   Brightly shone the moon that night,
   Though the frost was cruel,
   When a poor man came in sight,
   Gath'ring winter fuel.

King Wenceslas
 by Pauline Baynes (Living artist)

2. "Hither, page, and stand by me,
   If thou knowest it, telling,
   Yonder peasant, who is he?
   Where and what his dwelling?"
   "Sire, he lives a good league hence,
   Underneath the mountain,
   Right against the forest fence,
   By St. Agnes' fountain."

3. "Bring me flesh, and bring me wine,
   Bring me pine logs hither!
   Thou and I will see him dine,
   When we bear them thither."
   Page and monarch, forth they went,
   Forth they went together;
   Through the rude wind's wild lament
   And the bitter weather.

4. "Sire, the night is darker now,
   And the wind blows stronger;
   Fails my heart, I know not how;
   I can go no longer."
   "Mark my footsteps, good my page,
   Tread thou in them boldly:
   Thou shalt find the winter's rage
   Freeze thy blood less coldly."

5. In his master's steps he trod
   Where the snow lay dinted;
   Heat was in the very sod
   Which the saint had printed.
   Therefore, Christian men, be sure,
   Wealth or rank possessing,
   Ye who now will bless the poor,
   Shall yourselves find blessing.

Away in a Manger

1. Away in a manger, no crib for a bed,
   The little Lord Jesus laid down his
   sweet head.
   The stars in the sky looked down
   where he lay,
   The little Lord Jesus, asleep on the hay.

2. The cattle are lowing, the baby awakes,
   But little Lord Jesus, no crying
   he makes.
   I love thee, Lord Jesus, look down from
   the sky,
   And stay by my cradle till morning is nigh.

 Birth of Christ
by JOSIP GENERALIC (Living artist)

3. Be near me, Lord Jesus; I ask thee to stay
    Close by me forever, and love me, I pray.
    Bless all the dear children in thy tender care,
    And take us to heaven to live with thee there.

The Holly and the Ivy

1. The holly and the ivy,
   When they are both full grown,
   Of all the trees that are in the wood,
   The holly bears the crown.

   The rising of the sun
   And the running of the deer,
   The playing of the merry organ,
   Sweet singing in the choir.

Christmas Morning
 by THOMAS FALCON MARSHALL (1818–78)

2. The holly bears a blossom,
   As white as the lily flower,
   And Mary bore sweet Jesus Christ
   To be our sweet Savior. *Chorus*

3. The holly bears a berry,
   As red as any blood,
   And Mary bore sweet Jesus Christ
   To do poor sinners good. *Chorus*

4. The holly bears a prickle,
   As sharp as any thorn,
   And Mary bore sweet Jesus Christ
   On Christmas Day in the morn. *Chorus*

5. The holly bears a bark,
   As bitter as any gall,
   And Mary bore sweet Jesus Christ
   For to redeem us all. *Chorus*

6. The holly and the ivy,
   When they are both full grown,
   Of all the trees that are in the wood,
   The holly bears the crown. *Chorus*

O Little Town of Bethlehem

 Christmas Night at Bethlehem
by LUDOVIC ALLEAUME (1859–1938)

1. O little town of Bethlehem,
   How still we see thee lie!
   Above thy deep and dreamless sleep
   The silent stars go by.
   Yet in thy dark streets shineth
   The everlasting Light;
   The hopes and fears of all the years
   Are met in thee tonight.

2. O morning stars, together,
   Proclaim the holy birth!
   And praises sing to God the King;
   And peace to men on earth;
   For Christ is born of Mary,
   And gathered all above,
   While mortals sleep, the angels keep
   Their watch of wondering love.

3. How silently, how silently
   The wondrous gift is given!
   So God imparts to human hearts
   The blessings of his heaven.
   No ear may hear his coming,
   But in this world of sin,
   Where meek souls will receive him, still
   The dear Christ enters in.

4. O holy Child of Bethlehem,
   Descend to us, we pray;
   Cast out our sin, and enter in:
   Be born in us today!
   We hear the Christmas angels
   The great glad tidings tell;
   O come to us, abide with us,
   Our Lord Emmanuel.

The First Noel

 Angels Appearing to the Shepherds
by JACQUEMART DE HESDIN

1. The first Noel the Angel did say
   Was to certain poor shepherds in fields
     as they lay;
   In fields where they lay keeping their sheep
   On a cold winter's night that was so deep.
   Noel, Noel, Noel, Noel,
   Born is the King of Israel!

2. They looked up and saw a star,
   Shining in the east, beyond them far,
   And to the earth it gave great light,
   And so it continued both day and night.
   Chorus

3. This star drew nigh to the northwest,
   O'er Bethlehem it took its rest,
   And there it did both stop and stay,
   Right over the place where Jesus lay.
   Chorus

4. Then entered in those Wise Men three,
   Full reverently upon their knee,
   And offered there in his presence,
   Their gold and myrrh, and frankincense.
   Chorus

Song of the Crib

Christmas Eve
 by EDITH PAYNE (1875–1959)

1. Joseph dearest, Joseph mine,
   Help me cradle this child divine;
   God reward thee and all that's thine
   In paradise,
   So prays the Mother Mary.

   He came among us at Christmastide,
   At Christmastide in Bethlehem
   Men shall bring him from far and wide
   Love's diadem.
   Jesus, Jesus, Lo,
   He comes and loves and saves and frees us.

2. Gladly, dear one, Lady mine,
   I will cradle this child of thine,
   God's own light on us both shall shine
   In paradise,
   As prays the Mother Mary. *Chorus*

3. All shall come and bow the knee,
   Wise and happy their souls shall be,
   Loving such a divinity
   As all may see
   In Jesus, son of Mary. *Chorus*

Silent Night

1. Silent night, holy night!
   All is calm, all is bright
   Round yon Virgin Mother and Child;
   Holy Infant so tender and mild,
   Sleep in heavenly peace,
   Sleep in heavenly peace.

2. Silent night, holy night!
   Shepherds quake at the sight;
   Glories stream from heaven afar,
   Heavenly hosts sing Alleluia!
   Christ the Savior is born,
   Christ the Savior is born.

 The Virgin and Child Embracing
by Sassoferato (1609–85)

3. Silent night, holy night!
   Son of God, love's pure light;
   Radiance beams from thy holy face,
   With the dawn of redeeming grace;
   Jesus, Lord, at thy birth,
   Jesus, Lord, at thy birth.

It Came upon a Midnight Clear

1. It came upon a midnight clear,
   That glorious song of old,
   From angels bending near the earth
   To touch their harps of gold:

   "Peace on earth, good will to men,
   From heaven's all-gracious King!"
   The world in solemn stillness lay
   To hear the angels sing.

Music-making Angels by circle of
BERNARDINO LUINI (1475–1531)

2. Yet with the woes of sin and strife
   The world has suffered long;
   Beneath the angel's strain have rolled
   Two thousand years of wrong;
   And man, at war with man, hears not
   The love song which they bring:
   O hush the noise, ye men of strife,
   And hear the angels sing!

3. For lo! the days are hastening on,
   By prophet-bards foretold,
   When, with the ever-circling years,
   Comes round the Age of Gold;
   When peace shall over all the earth
   Its ancient splendors fling,
   And the whole world give back the song
   Which now the angels sing.

I Saw Three Ships

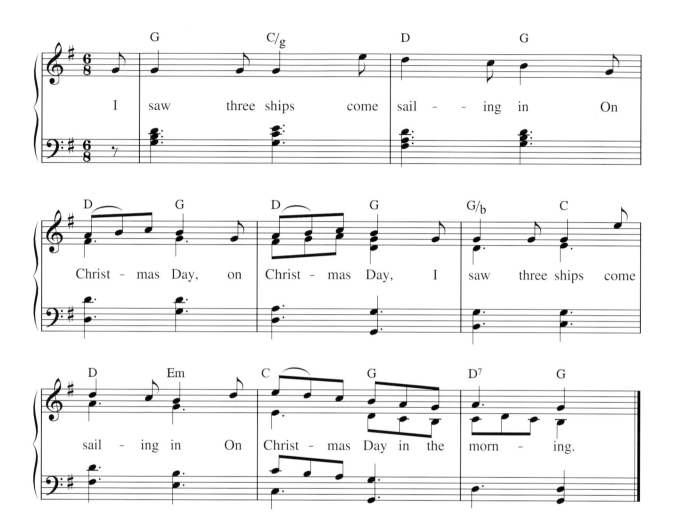

1. I saw three ships come sailing in
   On Christmas Day, on Christmas Day,
   I saw three ships come sailing in
   On Christmas Day in the morning.

2. And what was in those ships all three
   On Christmas Day, on Christmas Day?
   And what was in those ships all three
   On Christmas Day in the morning?

Following the Stars
 Illustration from the *Livre des
Merveilles* (compiled in 1351)

3. Our Savior Christ and his lady
   On Christmas Day, on Christmas Day,
   Our Savior Christ and his lady
   On Christmas Day in the morning.

4. And all the bells on earth shall ring
   On Christmas Day, on Christmas Day,
   And all the bells on earth shall ring
   On Christmas Day in the morning.

5. And all the souls on earth shall sing
   On Christmas Day, on Christmas Day,
   And all the souls on earth shall sing
   On Christmas Day in the morning.

We wish you a Merry Christmas

1. We wish you a merry Christmas,
   We wish you a merry Christmas,
   We wish you a merry Christmas,
   And a happy New Year!

   Glad tidings we bring
   To you and your kin,
   We wish you a merry Christmas,
   And a happy New Year!

2. Now bring us some figgy pudding,
   Now bring us some figgy pudding,
   Now bring us some figgy pudding,
   And bring it out here! *Chorus*

3. For we all like figgy pudding,
   For we all like figgy pudding,
   For we all like figgy pudding,
   So bring it out here! *Chorus*

 19th-century Christmas card

4. And we won't go until we get some,
   And we won't go until we get some,
   And we won't go until we get some,
   So bring it out here! *Chorus*

ACKNOWLEDGMENTS

The publisher would like to thank the following for their kind permission to reproduce their photographs:

AKG London Ltd: *Birth of Christ* by Josip Generalic, 1, 15; **Bridgeman Art Library, London:** Bibliothèque Nationale, Paris: Following the stars from the *Livre de Merveilles* by Jean le Long d'Ypres, 29; Bibliothèque Royale de Belgique, Brussels: Angels appearing to the shepherds from *Tres Belle Heures du Duc de Berry*, by Jacquemart de Hesdin, 21; Library of Congress, Washington D.C.: *Christmas Eve 1878* by J. Latham, 7; Musée des Beaux Arts, Angers, France: *Christmas Night at Bethlehem*, 1893 by Ludovic Alleaume, 19; The Makins Collection: *The Angel of the Trumpet* by Sir Edward Burne-Jones, 11; Private Collection: *Christmas Eve* by Edith Payne, 7; Private Collection: *King Wenceslas* by Pauline Baynes, 3, 13; Private Collection: *Three Kings* by Linda Benton, 9; Private Collection/Christopher Wood Gallery, London: *Christmas Morning*, 1865 by Thomas Falcon Marshall, 4, 17; **Christie's Images:** Music-making Angels; a fragment by the circle of Bernardino Luini, 2, 27; **National Gallery, London:** *The Virgin and Child Embracing*, by Sassoferato, 25; **Courtesy of the Trustees of the V&A:** Father Christmas and Children, 31.

Jacket: **The Bridgeman Art Library, London:** The Makins Collection: *The Angel of the Trumpet* by Sir Edward Burne-Jones, front, back; Private Collection: *King Wenceslas* (detail), by Pauline Baynes, inside front; Private Collection/Christopher Wood Gallery, London: *Christmas Morning*, (detail), 1865 by Thomas Falcon Marshall, inside back.

Dorling Kindersley would like to thank Chris Fraser for checking the music, and Claire Watson and Jane Thomas for design assistance.